Rübáiyát of Omar Khayyám

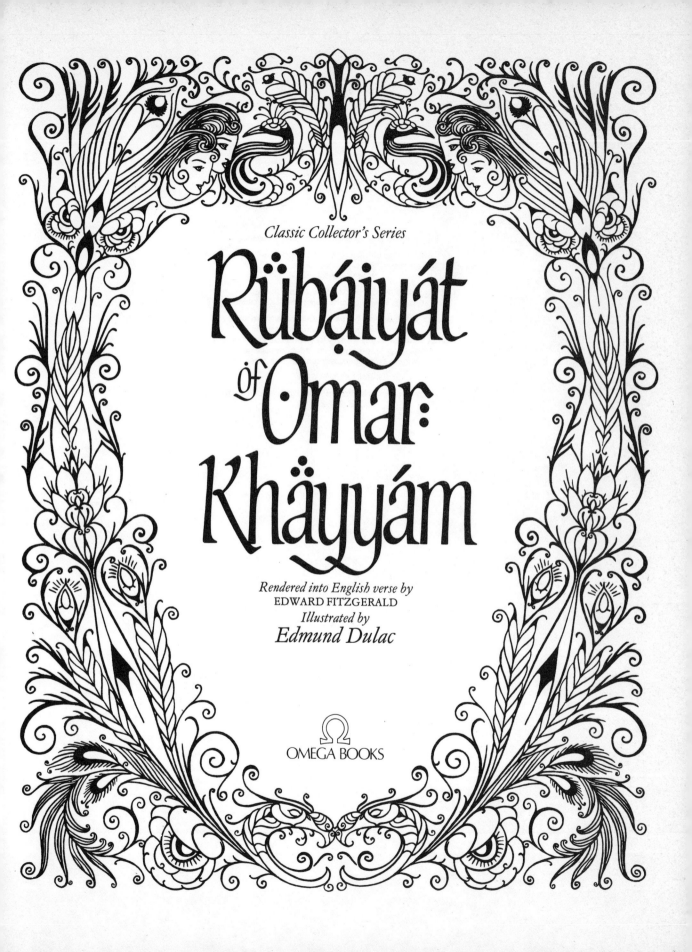

Classic Collector's Series

Rúbáiyát
Of Omar
Khäyyám

Rendered into English verse by
EDWARD FITZGERALD

Illustrated by
Edmund Dulac

OMEGA BOOKS

First published in 1909 by Hodder and Stoughton.

This edition published 1985 by Omega Books Ltd,
1 West Street, Ware, Hertfordshire, under licence
from the proprietor.

Copyright © 1983 this edition Hodder and Stoughton Ltd.
Illustrations by Edmund Dulac copyright M.G. Anderson.

ISBN 1 85007 061 X

Printed and bound in Spain by Printer Industria Grafica SA, Barcelona.
D.L.B. 25362-1985

ILLUSTRATIONS

ILLUSTRATIONS

Look to the blowing Rose about us---" Lo,
Laughing," she says, " into the world I blow :
   At once the silken tassel of my Purse
Tear, and its Treasure on the Garden throw."

XV

The Palace that to Heav'n his pillars threw,
And Kings the forehead on his threshold drew---
   I saw the solitary Ringdove there,
And " Coo, coo, coo," she cried ; and " Coo, coo, coo."

XX

For some we loved, the loveliest and the best
That from his Vintage rolling Time has prest,
   Have drunk their Cup a Round or two before,
And one by one crept silently to rest.

XXII

ILLUSTRATIONS

Alike for those who for TO-DAY prepare,
And those that after some TO-MORROW stare,
  A Muezzín from the Tower of Darkness cries,
"Fools ! your Reward is neither Here nor There !"

XXVII

And hidden by the sleeve of Night and Morn.

XXXVI

For I remember stopping by the way
To watch a Potter thumping his wet Clay :
  And with its all-obliterated Tongue
It murmur'd---"Gently, Brother, gently, pray !"

XL

Do you, within your little hour of Grace,
The waving Cypress in your arms enlace,
  Before the Mother back into her arms
Fold, and dissolve you in a last embrace.

XLIV

ILLUSTRATIONS

So when at last the Angel of the drink
Of Darkness finds you by the river-brink,
    And, proffering his Cup, invites your Soul
Forth to your Lips to quaff it---do not shrink.

XLVI

Oh, plagued no more with Human or Divine,
To-morrow's tangle to itself resign,
    And lose your fingers in the tresses of
The Cypress-slender Minister of Wine.

LV

You know, my Friends, how bravely in my House
For a new Marriage I did make Carouse.

LVII

Came shining through the Dusk an Angel Shape

LX

ILLUSTRATIONS

The Revelations of Devout and Learn'd
Who rose before us, and as Prophets burn'd
   Are all but Stories, which, awoke from Sleep
They told their fellows, and to Sleep return'd.

LXVIII

But that is but a Tent wherein may rest
A Sultan to the realm of Death addrest ;
   The Sultan rises, and the dark Ferrásh
Strikes, and prepares it for another guest.

LXX

Oh Thou, who Man of baser Earth didst make.

LXXXVIII

ILLUSTRATIONS

Yet Ah, that Spring should vanish with the Rose !
That Youth's sweet-scented manuscript should close !
  The Nightingale that in the branches sang,
Ah whence, and whither flown again, who knows ?

CIV

  And in your joyous errand reach the spot
Where I made One---turn down an empty Glass !

CX

I

WAKE! For the Sun behind yon Eastern height
Has chased the Session of the Stars from Night;
    And, to the field of Heav'n ascending, strikes
The Sultán's Turret with a Shaft of Light.

II

Before the phantom of False morning died,
Methought a Voice within the Tavern cried,
    "When all the Temple is prepared within,
Why lags the drowsy Worshipper outside?"

III

And, as the Cock crew, those who stood before
The Tavern shouted---"Open then the door !
   You know how little while we have to stay,
And, once departed, may return no more."

IV

Now the New Year reviving old Desires,
The thoughtful Soul to Solitude retires,
   Where the WHITE HAND OF MOSES on the
      Bough
Puts out, and Jesus from the ground suspires.

V

Iram indeed is gone with all his Rose,
And Jamshýd's Sev'n-ring'd Cup where no one
      knows ;
  But still a Ruby gushes from the Vine,
And many a Garden by the Water blows.

VI

And David's lips are lockt ; but in divine
High-piping Péhlevi, with "Wine ! Wine ! Wine !
  Red Wine !"---the Nightingale cries to the Rose
That sallow cheek of hers to incarnadine.

QUATRAIN LXXII

QUATRAIN I

VII

Come, fill the Cup, and in the fire of Spring
Your Winter-garment of Repentance fling :
    The Bird of Time has but a little way
To flutter---and the Bird is on the Wing.

VIII

Whether at Naishápúr or Babylon,
Whether the Cup with sweet or bitter run,
    The Wine of Life keeps oozing drop by drop,
The Leaves of Life keep falling one by one.

IX

Morning a thousand Roses brings, you say ;
Yes, but where leaves the Rose of yesterday ?
   And this first Summer month that brings the Rose
Shall take Jamshýd and Kaikobád away.

X

Well, let it take them ! What have we to do
With Kaikobád the Great, or Kaikhosrú ?
   Let Rustum cry "To Battle !" as he likes,
Or Hátim Tai "To Supper !"---heed not you.

XI

With me along the strip of Herbage strown
That just divides the desert from the sown,
    Where name of Slave and Sultán is forgot---
And Peace to Máhmúd on his golden Throne !

XII

Here with a little Bread beneath the Bough,
A Flask of Wine, a Book of Verse---and Thou
    Beside me singing in the Wilderness---
Oh, Wilderness were Paradise enow !

XIII

Some for the Glories of This World; and some
Sigh for the Prophet's Paradise to come;
    Ah, take the Cash, and let the promise go,
Nor heed the music of a distant Drum!

XIV

Were it not Folly, Spider-like to spin
The Thread of present Life away to win---
    What? for ourselves, who know not if we shall
Breathe out the very Breath we now breathe in!

XV

Look to the blowing Rose about us---"Lo,
Laughing," she says, "into the world I blow:
  At once the silken tassel of my Purse
Tear, and its Treasure on the Garden throw."

XVI

For those who husbanded the Golden grain,
And those who flung it to the winds like Rain,
  Alike to no such aureate Earth are turn'd
As, buried once, Men want dug up again.

XVII

The Worldly Hope men set their Hearts upon
Turns Ashes---or it prospers ; and anon,
　　Like Snow upon the Desert's dusty Face,
Lighting a little hour or two---was gone.

XVIII

Think, in this batter'd Caravanserai,
Whose Portals are alternate Night and Day,
　　How Sultán after Sultán with his Pomp
Abode his destin'd Hour, and went his way.

XIX

They say the Lion and the Lizard keep
The Courts where Jamshýd gloried and drank deep:
   And Bahrám, that great Hunter---the Wild Ass
Stamps o'er his Head, but cannot break his Sleep.

XX

The Palace that to Heav'n his pillars threw,
And Kings the forehead on his threshold drew---
   I saw the solitary Ringdove there,
And " Coo, coo, coo," she cried ; and " Coo, coo,
    coo."

XXI

Ah, my Belovéd, fill the Cup that clears
To-DAY of past Regret and future Fears :
    To-morrow !---Why, To-morrow I may be
Myself with Yesterday's Sev'n thousand Years.

XXII

For some we loved, the loveliest and the best
That from his Vintage rolling Time has prest,
    Have drunk their Cup a Round or two before,
And one by one crept silently to rest.

QUATRAIN XI

QUATRAIN XII

QUATRAIN XV

QUATRAIN XX

XXIII

And we, that now make merry in the Room
They left, and Summer dresses in new bloom,
    Ourselves must we beneath the Couch of Earth
Descend, ourselves to make a Couch---for whom ?

XXIV

I sometimes think that never blows so red
The Rose as where some buried Cæsar bled ;
    That every Hyacinth the Garden wears
Dropt in her Lap from some once lovely Head.

XXV

And this delightful Herb whose living Green
Fledges the River's Lip on which we lean---
   Ah, lean upon it lightly ! for who knows
From what once lovely Lip it springs unseen !

XXVI

Ah, make the most of what we yet may spend,
Before we too into the Dust descend ;
   Dust into Dust, and under Dust, to lie,
Sans Wine, sans Song, sans Singer, and---sans End !

XXVII

Alike for those who for TO-DAY prepare,
And those that after some TO-MORROW stare,
  A Muezzin from the Tower of Darkness cries,
"Fools! your Reward is neither Here nor There!"

XXVIII

Another Voice, when I am sleeping, cries,
"The Flower should open with the Morning skies."
  And a retreating Whisper, as I wake---
"The Flower that once has blown for ever dies."

XXIX

Why, all the Saints and Sages who discuss'd
Of the Two Worlds so learnedly, are thrust
    Like foolish Prophets forth; their Words to
      Scorn
Are scatter'd, and their Mouths are stopt with Dust.

XXX

Myself when young did eagerly frequent
Doctor and Saint, and heard great argument
    About it and about: but evermore
Came out by the same door as in I went.

XXXI

With them the seed of Wisdom did I sow,
And with my own hand wrought to make it grow:
   And this was all the Harvest that I reap'd---
"I came like Water, and like Wind I go."

XXXII

Into this Universe, and *Why* not knowing,
Nor *Whence*, like Water willy-nilly flowing:
   And out of it, as Wind along the Waste,
I know not *Whither*, willy-nilly blowing.

XXXIII

What, without asking, hither hurried *Whence*?
And, without asking, *Whither* hurried hence!
    Ah, contrite Heav'n endowed us with the Vine
To drug the memory of that insolence!

XXXIV

Up from Earth's Centre through the Seventh Gate
I rose, and on the Throne of Saturn sate,
    And many Knots unravel'd by the Road;
But not the Master-knot of Human Fate.

XXXV

There was the Door to which I found no Key:
There was the Veil through which I could not see:
  Some little talk awhile of ME and THEE
There was---and then no more of THEE and ME.

XXXVI

Earth could not answer : nor the Seas that mourn
In flowing Purple, of their Lord forlorn ;
  Nor Heaven, with those eternal Signs reveal'd
And hidden by the sleeve of Night and Morn.

XXXVII

Then of the THEE IN ME who works behind
The Veil of Universe I cried to find
    A Lamp to guide me through the darkness; and
Something then said---" an Understanding blind."

XXXVIII

Then to the Lip of this poor earthen Urn
I lean'd, the secret Well of Life to learn :
    And Lip to Lip it murmur'd---"While you live,
Drink !---for, once dead, you never shall return."

QUATRAIN XXII

QUATRAIN XXVII

QUATRAIN XXXVI

QUATRAIN XL

XXXIX

I think the Vessel, that with fugitive
Articulation answer'd, once did live,
   And drink ; and that impassive Lip I kiss'd,
How many Kisses might it take---and give !

XL

For I remember stopping by the way
To watch a Potter thumping his wet Clay :
   And with its all-obliterated Tongue
It murmur'd---"Gently, Brother, gently, pray ! "

XLI

For has not such a Story from of Old
Down Man's successive generations roll'd
 Of such a clod of saturated Earth
Cast by the Maker into Human mould?

XLII

And not a drop that from our Cups we throw
On the parcht herbage but may steal below
 To quench the fire of Anguish in some Eye
There hidden---far beneath, and long ago.

XLIII

As then the Tulip for her wonted sup
Of Heavenly Vintage lifts her chalice up,
   Do you, twin offspring of the soil, till Heav'n
To Earth invert you like an empty Cup.

XLIV

Do you, within your little hour of Grace,
The waving Cypress in your Arms enlace,
   Before the Mother back into her arms
Fold, and dissolve you in a last embrace.

XLV

And if the Cup you drink, the Lip you press,
End in what All begins and ends in—Yes ;
   Imagine then you *are* what heretofore
You *were*—hereafter you shall not be less.

XLVI

So when at last the Angel of the drink
Of Darkness finds you by the river-brink,
   And, proffering his Cup, invites your Soul
Forth to your Lips to quaff it—do not shrink.

XLVII

And fear not lest Existence closing *your*
Account, should lose, or know the type no more ;
   The Eternal Sáki from that Bowl has pour'd
Millions of Bubbles like us, and will pour.

XLVIII

When You and I behind the Veil are past,
Oh but the long long while the World shall last,
   Which of our Coming and Departure heeds
As much as Ocean of a pebble-cast.

XLIX

One Moment in Annihilation's Waste,
One Moment, of the Well of Life to taste---
   The Stars are setting, and the Caravan
Draws to the Dawn of Nothing---Oh make haste!

L

Would you that spangle of Existence spend
About THE SECRET---quick about it, Friend!
   A Hair, they say, divides the False and True---
And upon what, prithee, does Life depend?

LI

A Hair, they say, divides the False and True ;
Yes ; and a single Alif were the clue,
    Could you but find it, to the Treasure-house,
And peradventure to THE MASTER too ;

LII

Whose secret Presence, through Creation's veins
Running, Quicksilver-like eludes your pains :
    Taking all shapes from Máh to Máhi ; and
They change and perish all---but He remains ;

LIII

A moment guess'd---then back behind the Fold
Immerst of Darkness round the Drama roll'd
   Which, for the Pastime of Eternity,
He does Himself contrive, enact, behold.

LIV

But if in vain, down on the stubborn floor
Of Earth, and up to Heav'n's unopening Door,
   You gaze To-day, while You are You---how then
To-morrow, You when shall be You no more?

QUATRAIN XLIV

QUATRAIN XLVI

QUATRAIN LV

QUATRAIN LVII

LV

Oh, plagued no more with Human or Divine,
To-morrow's tangle to itself resign,
    And lose your fingers in the tresses of
The Cypress-slender Minister of Wine.

LVI

Waste not your Hour, nor in the vain pursuit
Of This and That endeavour and dispute ;
    Better be merry with the fruitful Grape
Than sadden after none, or bitter, Fruit.

LVII

You know, my Friends, how bravely in my House
For a new Marriage I did make Carouse:
    Divorced old barren Reason from my Bed,
And took the Daughter of the Vine to Spouse.

LVIII

For " Is " and " Is-NOT " though with Rule and
       Line,
And " UP-AND-DOWN " by Logic I define,
    Of all that one should care to fathom, I
Was never deep in anything but---Wine.

LIX

Ah, but my Computations, People say,
Have squared the Year to human compass, eh?
   If so, by striking from the Calendar
Unborn To-morrow, and dead Yesterday.

LX

And lately, by the Tavern Door agape,
Came shining through the Dusk an Angel Shape
   Bearing a Vessel on his Shoulder; and
He bid me taste of it; and 'twas---the Grape!

LXI

The Grape that can with Logic absolute
The Two-and-Seventy jarring Sects confute :
 The sovereign Alchemist that in a trice
Life's leaden metal into Gold transmute :

LXII

The mighty Mahmúd, Allah-breathing Lord,
That all the misbelieving and black Horde
 Of Fears and Sorrows that infest the Soul
Scatters before him with his whirlwind Sword.

LXIII

Why, be this Juice the growth of God, who dare
Blaspheme the twisted tendril as a Snare ?
　　A Blessing, we should use it, should we not ?
And if a Curse---why, then, Who set it there ?

LXIV

I must abjure the Balm of Life, I must,
Scared by some After-reckoning ta'en on trust,
　　Or lured with Hope of some Diviner Drink,
When the frail Cup is crumbled into Dust !

LXV

If but the Vine and Love-abjuring Band
Are in the Prophet's Paradise to stand,
   Alack, I doubt the Prophet's Paradise
Were empty as the hollow of one's Hand.

LXVI

Oh threats of Hell and Hopes of Paradise
One thing at least is certain—*This* Life flies:
   One thing is certain and the rest is Lies;
The Flower that once is blown for ever dies.

LXVII

Strange, is it not ? that of the myriads who
Before us pass'd the door of Darkness through
   Not one returns to tell us of the Road,
Which to discover we must travel too.

LXVIII

The Revelations of Devout and Learn'd
Who rose before us, and as Prophets burn'd,
   Are all but Stories, which, awoke from Sleep
They told their fellows, and to Sleep return'd.

LXIX

Why, if the Soul can fling the Dust aside,
And naked on the Air of Heaven ride,
   Is 't not a shame---is 't not a shame for him
So long in this Clay suburb to abide !

LXX

But that is but a Tent wherein may rest
A Sultan to the realm of Death addrest ;
   The Sultan rises, and the dark Ferrásh
Strikes, and prepares it for another guest.

QUATRAIN LX

QUATRAIN LXVIII

QUATRAIN LXX

QUATRAIN LXXXVIII

LXXI

I sent my Soul through the Invisible,
Some letter of that After-life to spell:
    And after many days my Soul return'd
And said, "Behold, Myself am Heav'n and
        Hell":

LXXII

Heav'n but the Vision of fulfill'd Desire,
And Hell the Shadow of a Soul on fire,
    Cast on the Darkness into which Ourselves,
So late emerg'd from, shall so soon expire.

LXXIII

We are no other than a moving row
Of visionary Shapes that come and go
    Round with this Sun-illumin'd Lantern held
In Midnight by the Master of the Show ;

LXXIV

Impotent Pieces of the Game he plays
Upon this Chequer-board of Nights and Days ;
    Hither and thither moves, and checks, and slays ;
And one by one back in the Closet lays.

LXXV

The Ball no question makes of Ayes and Noes,
But Right or Left as strikes the Player goes ;
    And He that toss'd you down into the Field,
He knows about it all---HE knows---HE knows !

LXXVI

The Moving Finger writes ; and, having writ,
Moves on : nor all your Piety nor Wit
    Shall lure it back to cancel half a Line,
Nor all your Tears wash out a Word of it.

LXXVII

For let Philosopher and Doctor preach
Of what they will, and what they will not---each
    Is but one Link in an eternal Chain
That none can slip, nor break, nor over-reach.

LXXVIII

And that inverted Bowl we call The Sky,
Whereunder crawling coop'd we live and die,
    Lift not your hands to *It* for help---for It
As impotently rolls as you or I.

LXXIX

With Earth's first Clay They did the Last Man
    knead,
And there of the Last Harvest sow'd the Seed:
    And the first Morning of Creation wrote
What the Last Dawn of Reckoning shall read.

LXXX

Yesterday *This* Day's Madness did prepare:
To-morrow's Silence, Triumph, or Despair:
    Drink! for you know not whence you came,
        nor why:
Drink! for you know not why you go, nor where.

LXXXI

I tell you this---When, started from the Goal,
Over the flaming shoulders of the Foal
   Of Heav'n Parwin and Mushtari they flung,
In my predestin'd Plot of Dust and Soul

LXXXII

The Vine had struck a fibre: which about
If clings my Being---let the Dervish flout;
   Of my Base metal may be filed a Key,
That shall unlock the Door he howls without.

LXXXIII

And this I know: whether the one True Light,
Kindle to Love, or Wrath-consume me quite,
    One Flash of It within the Tavern caught
Better than in the Temple lost outright.

LXXXIV

What! out of senseless Nothing to provoke
A conscious Something to resent the yoke
    Of unpermitted Pleasure, under pain
Of Everlasting Penalties, if broke!

LXXXV

What ! from his helpless Creature be repaid
Pure Gold for what he lent us dross-allay'd---
   Sue for a Debt we never did contract,
And cannot answer---Oh the sorry trade !

LXXXVI

Nay, but, for terror of his wrathful Face,
I swear I will not call Injustice Grace ;
   Not one Good Fellow of the Tavern but
Would kick so poor a Coward from the place.

QUATRAIN CIV

QUATRAIN CX

LXXXVII

Oh Thou, who didst with pitfall and with gin
Beset the Road I was to wander in,
    Thou wilt not with Predestin'd Evil round
Emmesh, and then impute my Fall to Sin ?

LXXXVIII

Oh Thou, who Man of baser Earth didst make,
And ev'n with Paradise devise the Snake :
    For all the Sin the Face of wretched Man
Is black with---Man's Forgiveness give---and take !

*   *   *   *   *

LXXXIX

As under cover of departing Day
Slunk hunger-stricken Ramazán away,
   Once more within the Potter's house alone
I stood, surrounded by the Shapes of Clay.

XC

And once again there gathered a scarce heard
Whisper among them ; as it were, the stirr'd
   Ashes of some all but extinguisht Tongue,
Which mine ear kindled into living Word.

XCI

Said one among them---" Surely not in vain,
My Substance from the common Earth was ta'en,
    That He who subtly wrought me into Shape
Should stamp me back to shapeless Earth again ? "

XCII

Another said---" Why, ne'er a peevish Boy
Would break the Cup from which he drank in Joy;
    Shall He that of his own free Fancy made
The Vessel, in an after-rage destroy ! "

XCIII

None answer'd this ; but after silence spake
Some Vessel of a more ungainly Make ;
   "They sneer at me for leaning all awry;
What ! did the Hand then of the Potter shake?"

XCIV

Thus with the Dead as with the Living, *What?*
And *Why?* so ready, but the *Wherefor* not,
   One on a sudden peevishly exclaim'd,
"Which is the Potter, pray, and which the Pot?"

XCV

Said one—" Folks of a surly Master tell,
And daub his Visage with the Smoke of Hell ;
   They talk of some sharp Trial of us—Pish !
He 's a Good Fellow, and 'twill all be well."

XCVI

" Well," said another, " Whoso will, let try,
My Clay with long oblivion is gone dry :
   But fill me with the old familiar Juice,
Methinks I might recover by-and-bye ! "

XCVII

So while the Vessels one by one were speaking,
One spied the little Crescent all were seeking :
    And then they jogg'd each other, " Brother !
        Brother !
Now for the Porter's shoulder-knot a-creaking ! "
    *   *   *   *   *

XCVIII

Ah, with the Grape my fading Life provide,
And wash my Body whence the Life has died,
    And lay me, shrouded in the living Leaf,
By some not unfrequented Garden-side.

XCIX

Whither resorting from the vernal Heat
Shall Old Acquaintance Old Acquaintance greet,
   Under the Branch that leans above the Wall
To shed his Blossom over head and feet.

C

Then ev'n my buried Ashes such a snare
Of Vintage shall fling up into the Air,
   As not a True-believer passing by
But shall be overtaken unaware.

CI

Indeed the Idols I have loved so long
Have done my credit in Men's eye much wrong
    Have drown'd my Glory in a shallow Cup,
And sold my Reputation for a Song.

CII

Indeed, indeed, Repentance oft before
I swore---but was I sober when I swore?
    And then and then came Spring, and Rose-in-
        hand
My thread-bare Penitence apieces tore.

CIII

And much as Wine has play'd the Infidel,
And robb'd me of my Robe of Honour---Well,
I often wonder what the Vintners buy
One-half so precious as the ware they sell.

CIV

Yet Ah, that Spring should vanish with the Rose!
That Youth's sweet-scented manuscript should
close!
The Nightingale that in the branches sang,
Ah whence, and whither flown again, who knows?

CV

Would but the Desert of the Fountain yield
One glimpse---if dimly, yet indeed reveal'd,
    Toward which the fainting Traveller might
        spring,
As springs the trampled herbage of the field !

CVI

Oh if the World were but to re-create,
That we might catch ere closed the Book of Fate,
    And make The Writer on a fairer leaf
Inscribe our names, or quite obliterate !

CVII

Better, oh better, cancel from the Scroll
Of Universe one luckless Human Soul,
    Than drop by drop enlarge the Flood that rolls
Hoarser with Anguish as the Ages roll.

CVIII

Ah Love! could you and I with Fate conspire
To grasp this sorry Scheme of Things entire,
    Would not we shatter it to bits—and then
Re-mould it nearer to the Heart's Desire!

CIX

But see !   The rising Moon of Heav'n again
Looks for us, Sweet-heart, through the quivering
        Plane :
  How oft hereafter rising will she look
Among those leaves---for one of us in vain !

CX

And when Yourself with silver Foot shall pass
Among the Guests Star-scatter'd on the Grass,
  And in your joyous errand reach the spot
Where I made One---turn down an empty Glass !

TAMÁM